Renunciation

Poems by
Corey Marks

D0068026

UNIVERSITY OF ILLINOIS PRESS

URBANA AND CHICAGO

Library of Congress Cataloging-in-Publication Data

Marks, Corey, 1970–

Renunciation : poems / by Corey Marks.

p.   cm.

ISBN 0-252-02581-4 — ISBN 0-252-06898-X (pbk.)

I. Title.

PS3563.A666R46   2000

811'.6—dc21   00-008321

1   2   3   4   5   C   P   5   4   3   2   1

Renunciation

The National Poetry Series

The National Poetry Series was established in 1978 to ensure the publication of five poetry books annually through participating publishers. Publication is funded by the late James A. Michener, The Copernicus Society of America, Edward J. Piszek, The Lannan Foundation, and the National Endowment for the Arts.

1999 Competition Winners

Tenya Darlington of Wisconsin, *Madame Deluxe*
> Selected by Lawson Inada, published by Coffee House Press

Eugene Gloria of Massachusetts, *Drivers at the Short-Time Motel*
> Selected by Yusef Komunyakaa, published by Viking Penguin

Corey Marks of Texas, *Renunciation*
> Selected by Philip Levine, published by the University of
> Illinois Press

Dionisio Martinez of Florida, *Climbing Back*
> Selected by Jorie Graham, published by W. W. Norton

Standard Schaefer of California, *Nova*
> Selected by Nick Piombino, published by Sun & Moon Press

Acknowledgments

Many poems in this volume previously appeared in the following publications, sometimes in different versions:

The Antioch Review:	"Portrait of a Child"
Black Warrior Review:	"A Partial History of Swine"
The Cream City Review:	"Elegy for the Music"
CutBank:	"Heart of Ash,"
	"What Fire Wants"
Indiana Review:	"Light"
New England Review:	"Gislebertus,"
	"Littoral,"
	"Minotaur"
New Virginia Review:	"Blind"
Orion:	"The Wrong Story"
The Paris Review:	"Sparrows,"
	"Solace," "American Monochrome,"
	"For Keats, after Keats,"
	"A Letter of Explanation,"
	"Renunciation"
Ruritan:	"Soup"

I am grateful to the writing communities at Warren Wilson College and the University of Houston for their support. Even more importantly, I wish to thank the readers who have provided invaluable help and encouragement during the drafting of this book: Christopher Bakken, Sharon Bryan, Ulric Dihle, Andrew Feld, Edward Hirsch, Richard Howard, Cynthia Macdonald, Christopher Matthews, Patty Seyburn, Pimone Triplett, and Larry Levis in memory. I owe a deep debt of gratitude as well to Philip Levine and the National Poetry Series for honoring my work.

*For my parents
and for Amy, my love*

Contents

one

Portrait of a Child

When I'm ready to think of something else, finally,
I think of wind that runs like a river along a river,
and trees bending into themselves with a will for breaking,
a will to break from the soil and leave the lap of the horsefield
where death has laid its head, its fire-red curls.

I think of the young painter who finds the body of a child,
drowned in the river and cast on stones that rattle
in the white hands of the water.

At first, the painter thinks all the right things.
He thinks of his own infant son.

But then he notices the child's beautiful blue lips
like the blue rim of a bowl, and the wine of its blood
spilled on a stone, and the dark loaves of its closed eyes
resting on the table of its face,

like the meal Christ rises over, sweeping his hands apart
while around the table the Apostles all lean against each other,
whispering, waiting, posing, even, for the thousands of painters
not yet born,

all but Judas, who looks away,
who has already broken the heavy bread and chews the grain,
not thinking of betrayal, of kissing sour wine from Christ's lips,

but of walking in a narrow street and hearing the song
of one bird that flew a hundred miles to rest in a tree
and pull its meal from a tent of worms.

The painter begins a portrait of the boy.
For a long time he stands beside the river, the brushes in a jar
near his hand, the sun turning lower in the sky,

and after a while he doesn't look at the child on the stones
but only at the boy lying in the soft bed of paint,
the dead boy at the end of his brush.

Then the boy by the water wakes
and climbs from the stones to the riverbank.
He walks to the painter and asks him, What are you painting?
You, the painter says, But you're dead.

No, the boy says, That boy is dead,
and he points to the painting.

The Butcher's Son

I would watch the butcher from behind a slatted fence
those mornings in the city where I first lived alone.
He'd pause in his yard to speak at his only child
before walking to his shop to crack open the day's carcasses,

before severing the simple lexicon of sinew and tendon
and bone, muttering the body's names while he worked
as though he wedged his knife between word
and thing, and split them, glistening, meaty,

to prove they were absolute. Each morning,
while his swollen-faced son turned endless circles
on a tricycle, the butcher would reach a finger
to trace the child's cheek wheeling by

and another circle would snap shut. The son,
who could not speak, or even listen,
spun the perimeter of his own wordlessness
through the days and evenings and into my sleepless dawns

when I would lean against the fence to see
something—anything—of the world not mine.
But then the butcher would step through the gate
—it's here I lose my place—and into the other city,

the wrong city, into the street outside the club
where J. Mascis twisted over his guitar

as though it had slammed into his chest, the hulking amps
pounding molecules of air into the crowd

so the sound opened in me with its furious touch,
like hands impatient and unsatisfied with what they found,
the hands that cut my mother and lifted me,
never born, into the world. The hands

that scrubbed me dry of her blood and smacked me
so I coughed a wail and split my ears to the tumult
of voices speaking everything I didn't know.
She said I was beautiful because of it, unbruised,

undistorted, and maybe I learned that word,
beautiful, because she knocked it against my skull
so long it finally jimmied its way in.
But as I wandered from the emptying club,

turning down a street where men pushed racks
of stripped and split cattle swaying like garments
that grazed one another's emptiness,
I finally wrested that word from her.

It's what I called the hush in my ears,
that stunning city the music had raised and abandoned,
vacant now but for the swirl of my blood
and my own steps tamping distantly,

as though someone turned away at the far corner
to leave me to myself. And now I can't help
but imagine the butcher behind me, after his gate
clacks shut against his son's muteness

and the tricycle's scrape. He turns from me
to a rack of meat, tilts a carcass towards
the narrow light. *Beautiful,* he says
to the dumb, dead flesh, and understands its silence,

the clearest thing that takes us from each other.

A Partial History of Swine

The Question

At night in the slop yard where swine
settle under tall yard lights cauterizing the dark,
the sound always comes back:

a mosquito's wire-thin insistence bending in
and out of their ears,
                              an unanswered question.

DeSoto Brings Thirteen Swine to the New World

The swine had never been on water before.
For weeks they heard it sloshing the hull,
creaking its weight against the boards
they rooted along for some scattered bit of slop,

but saw nothing they'd never seen before—
not the water's vast stranglehold on the ship,
nor the constant carnival of gulls—

just every other pig's dim ass
swaying its way toward the new world.

Microcosm

The swine won't drink from the trough.
They recognize something new

has breached the water,
a world without bones:

along the scummy bottom
larvae curl,
            little triggers.

Swine on Christ

What's he done that's so special?

Bleed? Die?

I've seen that trick before.

Transubstantiation

This little piggy went to market
where one name strips away as scalded skin,
and another is uncovered in the flesh itself,
marbled like fat in muscle.

This is where decisions are made about the body,
where the body becomes not its parts
but the butcher's sacrament:

Eat, and be whole.

••◡

The American Family Eats Pork

Each fork raises its own sliver of chop
    Rub pork with garlic
to an American mouth
    Dredge in flour
as the refrigerator murmurs a lament so constant
    Brown in heavy skillet
no one hears it.
    Heat thoroughly to avoid disease

••◡

The Answer

The pig says nothing, but whines
until the gunshot sucks the whine from its voice
under yellow light staining the slop yard with every brilliance
but illumination.

••◡

A Joke

A mosquito and a swine are on a boat
after three days of drifting.

Finally, the swine says,

> You must look at me and think *Ham* or *Tripe.*
> *Huff and puff. Trichinosis.* Whatever.
> But me, I've been thinking about History.

The mosquito says,

> *Soieee.*

Solace

It should be a denial, this morning,
the way winter's fallen across those hills so clearly

threatening too much light, a whiteness diffusing a negative
until whatever image it might hold,

trees paled and indistinct like a body's map of nerves,
blurs into a cess of light. Even the train—

where Kappus leans his head on the cabin's paneling,
his eyes narrowed to watch a young woman

thoughtlessly brush her fingers along her breast,
tracing the embroidered, interconnecting pattern of infinities

in the yellow fabric—even the train seems vague
in light and motion, a grayed seam shifting

among minutes and days and the change
of seasons. In Prague, hours before the train would leave,

he walked down one street where most homes
had been knocked out of this world by the war.

He knew the poet had lived here as a child,
and though he imagined that child curled in a window seat

watching a bee walk slow spirals along his arm
as outside the year's first snow began its multiplying variations,

he couldn't find which shattered house had held the boy.
Kappus sleeps on the train, finally, and the woman

disembarks, leaving only a faint impression in the worn cushion
across from him. He dreams Rilke

grown old into another life, no longer poet but a beekeeper
in a pear orchard. He dreams that in winter,

because he wanted to forget how enduring fails,
the poet edged briefly into the world

to drag white-box hives through wet snow
and into his house to hear in the waking bees' drone

what's infinite. Some crawled the twisted bed sheets,
or ceaselessly crossed the rim of a tall glass,

though most fretted circles in the air, describing brief,
dissolving constellations like properties of heaven

he couldn't own or lose. And when the poet slept,
snoring closer than ever to nothing,

a few bees entered his mouth and drew yellow stingers
delicately across his tongue. But Kappus, when he wakes,

wants some other solace, wants
light to erase everything but a street where he'll wait

as the woman in yellow steps like light across unblemished snow,
brilliant and whole without the world.

Elegy for the Music

When you listen to music,
after it's over, it's gone in the air.
You can never capture it again.
  —Eric Dolphy

Dolphy played
as though he didn't hear the end
coming, the music falling away, not yet—

just each note opening in his hands,
into the city, the room,
the stream of tape twisting the song

into itself; notes that could have been anything
played and in place, the song complete
and smaller now, almost thirty years—

he played as though each moment was endless
and changing, unclosable as a doorway
without a door opening into a city raised

right out of the heart of a continent.
But endings have a way of making themselves plain
as a slack-mouthed stormline that consumes sky

and starlight and intends to rain the dust
swirling in the streets to the ground.
In the midst of his set, he collapsed

into a blackness that opened out of him
and woke only once, near a hospital window.
He listened to his heart

and imagined it as a house, a man
wandering its rooms, shutting each door
with a final and quiet *click*,

and he began to hum an accompaniment
to its closing down—a quiet song behind his teeth
he didn't let out.

Heart of Ash

A boy crouched
In the low branches
Of a tree the sky above
Empty of flight

The boy said I want an apple
And he climbed down

He followed a road to the orchard
Where an old woman stood
Beneath the apple tree

She was his mother

There was no fruit on the tree
But round bee hives hung
From each branch
And silent there were no bees

She said
They were dying
He heard the bees in her voice

She put her hand to her belly
And the boy heard them now in her body
In the cage of her body

She said
But you haven't come to see me
And the boy looked away

She said Look
And she opened the skin of her arm
And bees flowed from her
Yellow blood spilling into her hand
The hundred moving wings

Couldn't fly the stream of bees
Fell to the ground
And then she was falling
Her body fell away

A cloud of bees it broke like rain
On the earth

But her heart remained in the air
It was a hive
Heart of paper heart of ash

And he took it from the air
Broke it open and inside was the apple
He put it to his mouth
And took the first stinging bite

Gislebertus

12th Century, St. Lazare Cathedral, Autun

He saw the damned in a stone and punished its surface away,
hammering lime into milling dust, shards, tics of blue static

flitting in each new groove and rent. In the small shop
outside the slowly rising cathedral, he worked the surface back

into itself, into a relief of Judgment he'd hang on the tympanum,
above the doors crowds would pass through to worship and be
    instructed.

He worked through hours, months of stone and dust, a slow
    cough
pulling his lungs, a tight pain winding his wrists, all for the
    anonymous

craft of turning stone into story. Until he paused
in the late sun sallowing the limestone before him, shaping itself

to figures he had carved: Christ, yes, and the Blessed, but also the
    Damned,
his glorious Damned twined with their punishments—a miser
    hung

by his own bag of money, an adulteress, her breasts gnawed by
    serpents,
a suicide whose neck is pinched between enormous fingers,
    slowing forever

the jugular's final spasm. As the last light sifted through the
    window,
as dust whorled to the dirt floor, he saw he had written

his version of pain into the story, *his* punishment, and knew
he could not let it go unclaimed. He set the chisel, raised the
    hammer,

knocked each letter into stone under Christ's feet—*Gislebertus
hoc fecit*—and gave a human name to everything that's damned.

two

A Letter of Explanation

By now, sir, you expect a second installment.
What novel is worth its ink if the hero's ship
never finishes sinking, if the cold tide
never tumbles him ashore into the provincial care
of two strolling shepherds?
But I'm not writing to beg leniency;

rather, to offer warning:
For so long I thought myself irreversibly
singular, but I've met another who shares
features almost indistinguishable
from my own and with them seeks to steal
everything I call my own.

When I first saw him, he was innocuous,
staring from a strategic corner in a café.
He learned to read lips so he could order
what *I* ordered. One by one, he acquired my habits
the way a lexicographer compiles a dictionary,
noting first the most rudimentary usages,

gradually adding nuance, context,
until his approximation was exhaustive.
What a performance! What unnerving self-reference.
His shadow-play followed me everywhere.
Once, my novel in its first flush upon the page,
I—we—took a train all night through the mountains,

to think, to be driven further inside my story.
I spoke to him then, my double, my shadow,
and he listened, attentive, all nods
and approving hums. The perfect audience.
Then he spoke. Imagine, never having seen one,
you find yourself before a mirror.

Shock, at first. An inability to fit your mind
around the clear fact of your outward self,
the stranger agape before you.
Soon, though, you tame a stray wisp of hair.
Check your teeth, the fit of your overcoat.
Imagine how others see you, what they miss.

The mirror becomes indispensable,
a page of reference to an aspect of yourself.
It pales before what I found in him.
He was the book, perfect and whole.
You see the cruelty in his disappearance.
I've returned to the mountains, scoured trains, villages.

So often I want to call his name,
but what name would I call? My own?
I've asked after him on the streets, in cafés, hotels.
I've described him, pointing to my own face.
I've seen the glances, shoulders turning away. I'm not blind
no matter how blind the world becomes to me.

You must understand my negligence,
why my ambitions are all postponed,
peering into the yawning waves.
The amputee who still feels the ache of a missing limb

knows nothing of my state. I do not feel an arm
still attached, but rather that it is elsewhere,

perched on a desk behind a door I've yet to find,
clutching a pen that descends a page
filled with waves of script—*my* script—,
conducting the body's business on its own.
I implore your patience, sir, and your caution,
for we are not always who we are.

American Monochrome

If I tell a story of America it will be with the needle
splitting Demuth's needle-pocked skin—how his blood blooms
in insulin as he hunches his shoulder to shield the syringe

from the crowds around him who stare into the arcs of acrobats
pinwheeling through the splayed open air of the circus tent.
Before the thumbstroke and glide he watches his blood fade

and thinks of the garden he wandered in Paris before he collapsed
and the weakness and craving became a disease, before it became
a word. The garden where another man knelt

in front of a wash of lilacs and coughed once, a dry, shallow
      cough . . .
Or I'll tell it with the watery fade of color from his brushpoint
into the melting flight of the acrobats, how the distant hand of
      one

becomes lost behind the yellow body of another and how,
as it passes into the other man's crotch, the hand dissolves
into the paper, into a forgiveness for desire, and not a denial,

not the precise denial in the incorruptible geometries
of his Lancaster, the razor-incised pencil line and oil, black
      windows
red buildings, black smokestacks speaking balloons of white
      smoke.

And if Demuth wanted to paint America, it was in the way a razor
is a roduction of slag and smoke calling out the emptiness
behind the black flattened windows, the hands and faces

and bodies vanished as though Demuth scorched his city
into the precision of machine, absolved of its makers,
and not in the way a sailor gently traces a razor along his arm,

inscribing the skin with a heart, with initials—*C* and *D* . . .
but he is simply color faded onto paper, a man grabbing his cock
and turning his arm toward the absent brushstroke. Even so,

if I'd bent closer, and if the guard hadn't told me sharply
to step back, I would have seen the lines carved in flesh welling
with blood . . . And the plume of blood washing into the clear
    syringe

has nothing to do with America, and everything
with the pale flowers Demuth painted when he was too weak
to leave his home—hyacinth, iris, zinnia, cinereria.

He would wake and swing to the edge of his bed, disentangling
from the sheets rumpled and stained only by sleeplessness
as his mother leaned just outside the room, watching

through the half-open door. He would reach for his brush
and the rough-surfaced paper and paint whatever brilliant
    measure
his mother had set beside him as he slept, stilling the flowers'

dissolution in water color, and making it clearer . . . But when
    Demuth

wandered the Paris garden he didn't think of the flowers, not yet,
but of how he could seduce America into his brushstroke.

And if I say the coughing man, too, thought of America, that he
    was writing
a country he'd never seen into a novel he never quite finished;
that when he returned to Prague his cough deepened, and he
    scrawled

when his larynx was fire: *The lilac—dying it drinks and goes on
    swilling;*
or even if I simply say when he left the garden he looked away
from Demuth's glance, and flicked a smear of dirt off his knee—

you must forgive me this distortion, this smudging of my story.
Let it fade the way Demuth's brushes bleed into his cups of water
as he finally turns away from the dissected air of the circus tent,

from the acrobats dressed in red and black and not in yellow,
    spinning
into each other's grasps. He packs the brushes and pocked tubes
and walks outside to pour the color-tainted water at the base

of a straw-strewn cage. And when he looks into the black bars
he feels himself dissolving, caving into the absence opening in his
    blood.
He reaches for the metal and thinks the cage waits for something
    new.

The Wrong Story

Roscommon County, Michigan, August 1995

I was tired of houses, tired of how a day
knocks itself against the walls like a stunned,
trapped bird. *That* day, the radio's fuzzy memory
of another August, fifty years gone,

recled its versions against the kitchen windows—
It ended the war, saved lives—and then another,
a survivor's testimony—*Heat swept through houses
miles beyond the blast, so dense*

*I was completely naked in its wake. How odd!
Where were my drawers and undershirt?
Where was my wife?* Until I couldn't listen
and closed the door on each story that wasn't enough.

I drove to a dirt road stripped though stands
of second-growth trees, and after I'd pulled
onto the weed-tousled shoulder, left the car
with its ticking engine, after I'd walked awhile

and been there awhile, the place began
its own broadcast: the woods amplifying uncertainty,
the cicada-song's ladder breaking mid-climb,
dust wavering between the narrow trees.

One sound still crackled from the woods' hush,
but I thought it just the approach of something human

wandering from the incessant highway.
I turned a little so not to see another's entrance.

But in the time it took to break my gaze
from where the noise welled, the instant ripened
into a pause, the way a breath breaks rushing syllables,
the ticking of language, and leans hard

into silence—like a bomb nosing the inevitable
the instant before it gives in to itself.
So when the bear broke from the woods
and turned to gaze at me along its rounded dark,

it was the wrong story, not the one I'd told myself.
This was something that shouldn't be here.
This was no one. This was nothing
but the unmeasured beat of eyes.

At first I couldn't hear beyond my heart
volleying cells through my skull,
couldn't hear bays and yelps chorusing
from the treeline. Fear quivered with definition,

in its brief measure. Its cause had a form,
a body so alive it tore the instant's meniscus,
and slid back into the trees. I want to tell
the right story, say I knew I wasn't the one at risk,

that I knew mine was a pale fear next to the survivor's
when he'd stared into the sudden brilliance
of his garden, a stone lantern engulfed
in more light than any flame it had borne before.

But in the woods, a pack of hounds erupted,
wiry gray shrapnel tracing the road
where the bear had paused, their noses translating
scents into motion. Around their necks,

small transistors signaled their position
toward the highway, where a man in a pick-up
tracked the displaced waves shocking the air
so he could get his bearings,

the way a bomber seeks his target in a city
scrolling below. Then, in dust swarming the road,
radio-waves fingered through my shirt
like a caress, a nauseated relief. Like complicity.

Light

Once I passed out and as I fell into my head's thrumming
I heard geese call, heading south,
and drew them with me until their sound
was the only sound, as though I'd snared them
in a collapsing net. And as I kicked through
those seconds locked tightly in my furious dreaming,

I ground my teeth so hard one chipped,
so that now a man has his fingers in my mouth, among those
     crowded,
crooked teeth I've tried to hide behind my lips so many years.
He places a small square of X-ray film, tells me to bite,
and steps away to the lead-lined barrier.
How easily the geese passed through me, like the X-ray,
like the world happening only to itself and not to me.

Years ago, I leaned against a doorframe
and a girl kissed me because my friend asked her; her mouth
opened, but I didn't kiss back. I held my lips
against her tongue until she stopped, and now
as the machine above me buzzes and I close my eyes to feel the
     light
move into my head,

she stands in a small kitchen
clasping a green glass full of tap-water, her husband of a year
shouting, his hand reaching into the air

as though he thinks to pull the house down on her,
the plaster ceiling, the old man upstairs washing his ragged mutt,
the one living thing he has left to love;

as though to pull the afternoon light through the walls,
to reveal her, change her, as though light alone
can transform a body and its life.
His fist falls across her mouth that opened so softly once,
and the ceiling seems to shiver in the pale light but holds.
For a moment she hears the old man singing to his dog.

She leaves to walk where the geese have finally gathered
on the river bank, and the dentist touches a drill bit to my broken
	tooth
to grind its roughness into smoke and dust. But the geese
know so easily how to leave, and launch
into the air and the wake of their honking.
Nothing now and maybe nothing years ago

I could do would stop his fist. It wasn't gentleness
that kept me from opening my mouth
and taking her tongue between my teeth, not desirelessness.
I was afraid of my mouth, those jumbled teeth,
afraid she would simply pass through me.
I didn't want to know the world didn't want me.

Blind

I know too little of blindness, here, near my grandfather
who rolls his eyes to see anything, anything
through the small holes of sight left to him.
I remember the blind girl who traced a circle

around her feet so they would be somewhere
she would know. Her father and I watched
from the river's edge as a snake slipped into the yard,
into the circle she'd drawn. The snake

brushed her ankle and she reached down to it.
She touched it where its back caught the sun. There was a grace
to her blindness, because she knew nothing else, a grace
my grandfather doesn't have. He lies in his bed,

his eyes flickering, looking at nothing
but the air, as though he watches for his breath
to unfold from his lungs and lift him out of everything he's
    known.
Or it's simpler than that: he wants to see

the pattern of the ceiling, to know he can still see
the shadow of rough paint in the room where he's slept
most of his life. And the swirl of paint looks to his nearly blind
    eyes
like wings, and so, he's a little more sure of his dying.

I believe the blind girl's father who told me some nights
she walks into the jungle, not so far he can't hear her,
but far enough to be gone, lost to him. He listens
to the small sounds she makes and waits

to see her pass between the trees and into the yellow
light of the bulb that fills the yard. And she knows
he's there, watching, and she wants him to be there.
She wants him to watch and not to see her.

The Clockmaker's Daughter

A child wanders into a wood
and follows a river's frozen course
through trees, through a constant wind
so harsh it scatters pine needles
into the air, startling a sentinel crow.
The child shades her eyes with a hand

to see the cawing's source. Her hand
is bare. She's not dressed for the wood,
or the cold, and is surprised by the crow,
by its warning, its splintering voice, coarse
yet sharp, pricking the hush like a needle
with the call for its flock to take to the wind.

The cry turns feeble in the wind
as the child listens, rubbing one hand
against the other. Her palms teem with needles
as they warm, and the cawing fails in the wood,
fading before it completes its course.
She wants to ask, *Why does the rooster crow*

to announce the morning, but never the crow?
But for answer she'd hear the wind,
gusting and hollow, and water, coursing
quietly below ice. Her hands'
thin, dry rustle. The wood
swallows its answers, and spits needles

instead, flocks of needles
perforating the air around the crow
and the child. A hush binds the wood,
strung through branches in a taut wind
as though tightened by an unseen hand—
the clockmaker's, say, who of course

prefers silence, the unquestioned course
of time, the way the sharp needle
of the ceaseless, persistent second-hand
ticks away each hour until the crow
emerges from the clock, and the girl winds
along her mechanical trail in the wood.

But she dreams another course—the crow
sweeping through pine needles in the wind
to her open hand, just as she knew it would.

For Keats, after Keats

i

Were I there, leaning against a London building's
filthy stonework, gazing by chance into a street
at the moment of *this* carriage's transit
from the city, its long exhalation toward Hampstead,

I'd watch the man clinging on the carriage-top
who stares at the driver's lash streaming in the air
as though each flick creates a new inscription
and not the trace of everything already undone.

This man, who doesn't understand the sun
whorled in sharp blue when he collapses, or the city's
fevered inversion, doesn't understand the gravity
until the carriage-top licks hard against his cheek.

I'd watch the moment when he begins his blur
toward imperceptibility, when the cough comes,
scrawling its way through his lungs, each spasm
a foul adjective describing the noun of his body,

though untranslatable, like the script of a child
who hasn't learned to write but writes anyway,
filling a page with interlacing loops
already shaped by his hand's shape, slanted

and crooked with what renders difference, makes
any word spiraling from his hand *his* word.
Only the child can tell what story's housed
in those sprawling ovals, and he remains

mute on the matter, bending close to the pen tip,
listening, in some small room notched in the city,
to the cut of each slow line against paper,
the immaculate sound of his body entering language.

ii

Perhaps the child's story is of a room—a room
as empty as his wide scrawl, where the walls
have been washed again with white, and its articles
emptied into the city crosshatched beyond the window:

a bed, rolled and burned in a Roman alleyway
under the disinterested eye of a policeman, fueled
by a trunk of books, pages bending back into themselves
in flames, scoured first of words, then matter.

But the child will lose his own story in time, no matter
how he shapes the words. He'll never be the poet,
but the one left with another's words, never be
the one who hunches in a room writing a letter

when light rears from the ache in his lungs
like an incomprehensible utterance, light streaming
as an imagined visitation, a form so bloated
with luminescence it must burst, and does

when the lesions nettling his lungs wane,
sharpening the room's lines: *it's only morning;*
and the dullard sun scrubs through the filthy windows.
Instead, the child will become the man

who copies the letter in legible script. One morning
he'll sit in his own cold room, his back to a window,
and stitch a row of X's over the name Keats
penned so certainly in his final letter—*I shall write to . . .*

He listens for the tick as the pen snaps each line
cross its opposite, listens as what was left undone
is undone, as outside the sun presses
like a faint and failing face against the glass.

iii

Were I that child, perhaps I would have laced
a different story into my chain of ovals, a story
I'd never have let go. Though more likely I too
would have diminished, sloughing my story's skin

to find myself at a desk mottled with Keats' papers,
the city leaning through the window at my shoulder.
I would have gazed mutely as my hand stitched over
the name in his letter with a coroner's imprecision.

But I never stared into the poet's unraveling,
never saw the final tangle of possibility still disturbing
the world as it came undone. My eyes blur
tracing the breathless cells Keats' words have become,

empty as a chain of loops inscribed across a page,
empty as his lungs, half consumed and blackened
when the doctors cracked his chest in autopsy
to look on the disease they'd misread.

Nerves, they had told him, as though something
so vague could write him out of the story.
His words are text and texture on paper, or are excised
in a simple row of X's, a last retraction of possibility.

I want to copy what's illegible, make it clear,
though only my own words curl in my hand. My story.
There's no recovery—not even in the doctor's words
as he fingers Keats' vein, months before death,

and ticks the skin with a scalpel, releasing blood
to streak along the poet's arm toward free fall,
toward the bodiless, unencumbered moment:
Don't write. Don't write again.

three

Renunciation

i

In evening light's splayed radiance,
in a field of scrub and vines hedging a river,
a boy found a black snake sunning itself.
When he crouched near, his face bloomed in its scales
so the snake's coils were crowded with his eyes.

I almost want to leave him there, dawning
with amazement, this boy dead centuries now
and hushed in weak soil, leave him before
he flares with too much certainty.
But like every moment, this one brims over.

ii

He'd dreamt of angels, arranged in slow descent
above the field, calling, and so he came
to meet them, to feel his soul quiver and strain
as they approached from a cracked sky with word
from Christ above. All day he waited.

A man stumbled past who always wept
outside the church, but wouldn't enter. At first
the villagers had thought he was a prophet.
They'd heard of such men, wandering the towns.
They'd waited for him to speak, to preach—but nothing.

The boy watched children by the river
who tossed mud in long, fraying arcs.
An older boy and girl ran, laughing,
toward a stand of ankle-thin pines,
glancing over their shoulders at what never followed.

A woman offered a loaf from a basket of bread
but the boy said no, turned his eyes from hers,
told her he couldn't eat until the angels arrived.
She waved his words off with a thrust of her hand
as though to knock the winged host to earth.

Staring at the stone-littered ground,
he saw a shadowed arc of wings pass.
Before he raised his head, a cawing gave away
the crow. Perhaps waiting wasn't enough.
He thought of prayer, intoning the thin peal

of his plea in the failing light, his voice probing,
a key to unlock the shell of sky above.
But what if it was the wrong key, and the sky
never opened, and the first piercing sweetness
never crossed, fluttering, into his world?

iii

For the boy, wonder is an impoverishment
because it hinges so uncertainly
between what's real and what's not, between
faith and illusion, between a room filled
with the luxury of material fact—

splintered knob of a saint's knuckle bone,
shroud stained with Christ's deathly features—
and an open field filled with proof of nothing
but river and crow and snake and the irritation
of human lives trailing through the light.

What if he never truly felt the comfort
a soul must be to the body that knows it's there?—
seasoning in fatty soup that makes it palatable,
the tang of immortality clinging to the tongue—
the way a monk, even when he doesn't

fold against a cobbled floor in prayer,
and instead bends to the body's work
of sustenance, feeding clamor-filled cells;
when he inclines a blade against the velvet
where an ear scrolls into a bull's sable neck,

the way even then the monk feels
the surety of his soul. But how? How?
The boy might even welcome the surety of *not*
having a soul, just to be sure of something,
the way my father was, centuries later,

exiting from an exhibit on Christ's life
onto Lake Shore Drive's tumult, beneath a sky
that looked gilded in its grimy, city-stained way,
infused with the luminescence of street lamps,
headlights and neon, with the minor fluorescent hells

of a thousand convenience stores, where some souls
waited all night for a few quarters

not to buy their way into heaven, but a little deeper
into their bodies' dull thrum. My father,
head tilted back, breath unfurling

in a crude, cursive arc, thought the sky
had the muted, quenched radiance of a painting
no one had taken the time to clean for years,
to brush century-old grime from gold-leaf.
Inside, he'd stood before such a painting:

Mary, dully crowned with what he knew
should be brilliance, bowing her head away
from the angel who hovers just above
in a field of gold, wings motionless,
ornamental. *They shouldn't look so still,*

my father had thought, leaning nearer,
studying the feathers for some telltale sign
that the painter hadn't gotten it entirely wrong.
When he'd touched one wing, briefly,
his finger came away mottled with dust.

That's the problem with God, he'd whispered then
to no one, or to the clinging dust on his finger
that had been something else before dust.
Then, because the museum guard had drifted
into another room, and God was too dead

to listen either to prayer or complaint,
he stopped whispering and sloughed the dust—
a quick flick of his thumb against finger—
and walked outside into the gilded city
on a lake gouged by a glacier's final clasp.

iv

It is nothing, the boy thought, but he could not
take his eyes off the coils. He felt
the first convection of something in his chest
like a red shimmer passing through an ember
before it flares into flame. He stared at the snake,

at its mosaicked images of himself, bleary,
smudged, but clearly him, caught as though
beneath glass, each face a beating moth
stupefied against an invisible wall.
Or no, not moths, but distant angels rising

toward him, bearing his own bleak,
wasted expression. But it wasn't enough to stay
swaddled in momentary awe, neither
believing nor not, wavering as on the cusp
of fire, incipient, neither flame

nor cinder. I want to say, *Don't wake up,*
tell him I would get on my knees and pray
to the very thing he wanted to dispel,
to the hush when the uncertain heart falls out
of time. But the boy goes on without me. He touches

the snake as though searching for a secret clasp
that would spring it open. But the snake writhes free,
contorting in the dust, shaping itself
like letters in a painting of Christ he'd knelt before,
words written above a winding vine

grown from Christ's pierced side, heavy,
straining with blood-red grapes ready
to burst into wine. Words he couldn't read
then or now. If only the shapes were fathomable
he thinks he'd understand the furious escape

—sentences, whole volumes inscribed
before his illiterate eyes. The flesh made word.
He looks away, at woven vines and grasses,
a fractured line of clouds, the distant pines.
Everything wells with a sense he cannot render.

He tries to shape the things he sees as sounds
but his tongue swells as though bitten, clotting his voice.
Still he won't relent. He follows the snake
to the riverbank. It pauses at the water
then slips its length into the blacker current.

v

Here is my version of the impoverished soul,
poor coal for which there is not enough breath
to stoke: midnight, blown out of his mind
on whatever it was he could afford, he fumbles
against a window without knowing it's a window,

framing himself. He can't keep his hands
off himself: they rove like eyes, searching
face, crotch, chest, ragged crown
of hair, as though to find a way to fit
shattered pieces into a forgotten pattern.

What amazement his fingers stumble over.
What grim ecstasy. And all the while
he calls out a prayer, the only one he knows,
tonguing words as though counting beads:
Oh man, oh man, oh God, oh man, oh no . . .

But I was taught there is only the world, only
crow and river and snake, and no soul.
My father gave me a stone and said, *Stone.*
He taught me words I've yet to learn to use
in any prayer, to praise the poorest wonder.

vi

Something's changed beneath the heavenless sky.
The boy watches the snake crossing water,
surging through the late sun's blazing sheen,
and he's quickened by what bursts inside his chest
like the sudden unfurling of a shroud from a body

that was never dead, only long lost in sleep.
And as the mourners would cease wailing, and stare
slack-jawed at the risen body, and wait
for some instruction in what next to believe,
so now the villagers come expectantly to the boy.

The woman selling loaves returns, her basket
empty, hungering for more than bread alone.
Then others—the old weeping man, a mother
with her sons, the girl of sixteen who runs
ahead of her lover so they won't arrive together.

A crowd has gathered. Even the crow settles near.
The boy begins to preach what isn't quite
and what will never exactly be gospel,
but close, something unwound from the same nest
of stories. He says, *The serpent is God's reversal*

mirrored on earth, shattered into a hundred
blackened scales, into an empire. He points
to the swift waterline as the serpent begins
its slow climb on the far bank. *Rejoice*
at the snake, for even in Evil can we see

God's presence. There can be no reflection,
no reversal, without an opposite.
He bends to grasp a stone between his feet.
Even so, we must hate the serpent. It seeks
to steal us from our Lord, to secret us

away in its coils. The serpent is our prison.
He weighs the stone, sharp along an edge.
His thumb relishes the sharpness. *Jesus says*
Whosoever does not hate his father
his mother, wife, children, brothers and sisters,

yes, even life itself, cannot be
Christ's disciple. That, he nods at the snake,
is both our brother and our keeper, the one
who keeps us from our Lord. By now the others
hold stones at ready. Now no amazement

is enough. When the snake shrugs its coils away,
shouldering upright not as an angel but a man,
nothing can stop the prophet and his crowd.
They cast their stones at what plainly stands
so abruptly human between them and God.

four

Minotaur

Once, from a window grimed by sleeping heads
lolling for long hours against the glass
on a bus that passed through mountains
between Quito and Cuenca,
I watched as mist yielded the startled face
of a bull tied by one horn to a stake.
The bull stood so close to the road you'd think
it must have seen a bus charge from the mist before.
But from the animal's stricken-wide eyes
taking in exactly what it didn't want to see,
it was all new. I almost didn't notice
the girl soothing the bull's neck with her palm
before the mist scoured them both blank.
My fellow passengers slept on in the quiet nave of the bus
until we stopped in a cobbled town square
where soldiers sat on their haunches, playing cards,
rifles rested against a fountain's rim.
Those of us awake heard the engine's idle pangs
and soldiers laughing beyond our squares of glass.

Some stories can't be kept behind the teeth,
like the one my father told me once
on a street corner in Chicago, waiting for a light.
The summer three years before I was born
he'd stood at the edge of Grant Park

and watched police march into crowding protesters,
beating with riot sticks as they pushed through.
One girl spun around, ran, not young enough
to be his daughter, but almost,
and he saw a black rod fall against her once,
twice, not stopping even as she fell.
Her eyes caught his and held so that now,
when she remembers being beaten,
she remembers my father's face most clearly—
how he stood beneath the trees bending so slightly
in a wind off Lake Michigan.

When a soldier walked the aisle of the bus,
looking carelessly over jumbled sacks,
a few chickens scrabbling to stand on bound legs,
this was something new. The rifle across his back
passed so near I could've grasped its barrel.
I still don't know how to explain this desire:
not for death, no, but for a moment when possibility
bristles so close it holds a shape in the air.
I wanted to make something happen,
to feel the world change a little beneath my palm.
Something to absolve my stare.
Something I'd tell, later, to someone who'd listen:
Crowds hurried through the square, vendors
called out their goods in high wail to pierce the clamor,
the soldier turned away, and my hand
spread toward his rifle because it could.
A gesture simple as the way a man at the front of a bus
flicks his fingers to tell the driver to stop,
or simple as the way my father rests his knuckle on a page

to hold his place when he looks from his book
and into the waves of air. The way a woman
in some small classroom, Evanston or Oak Park
or Gary, brushes aside a stray bang as she glances
over the rows of her students' small heads
to the far windows, and pauses in telling her story.

───

She sees a wind turn through the trees outside.
A man crosses the schoolyard, the trees bend,
and it returns so easily—how she fell beneath
the black wand and the breaking in her head.
She thinks of a new story to tell her students:
how Daedalus gave the Minotaur charcoal
and paper scrolls before closing the labyrinth.
How the Minotaur drew each boy and girl given to him.
He broke their necks below the strange, smooth faces
and they never fought, relinquishing themselves
as though they knew they were his and knew
he would take them. He drew each child, carefully,
his large hands tracing figures never really the same
as the wilted bodies on the floor, drew them continuously
through the undifferentiated days and nights
until they dissolved into bone and lines on paper.
Until he couldn't believe their faces, or stand
their difference, and unfurled the scrolls
to scour the drawings with thick charcoal so each face
mirrored his own—the heavy snout, the horns
curling up like smoke. And when one didn't give
itself away, and fought, slammed its narrow fingers
into his nostrils, his head bent back into the sound of breaking.

The teacher stands before a chalk-filled blackboard.
When she sees Theseus' face, it's my father's.

～

In the market square a vendor charred the thin flesh
of a bull's head over a cookfire, then tore
blackened meat into strips to be sold and eaten
and forgotten. On the bus, the soldier stepped
away from my hand, and the bristled moment
blurred into what didn't happen. All I'm left
is my tongue's inexactness, its conceit. Too late to say,
Look, so you'll see and there'll be no need for telling.
I'm like the woman telling her story,
or like my father telling his. Though he watched
a girl beaten, she never looked at him.
She buried her head in her arms and curled
against the grass. He stared and did nothing
but stand beneath the trees at the edge of Grant Park
wondering why he did nothing, and why
no one struck him. But he didn't tell me that—
he said a girl fell beneath a riot stick
and her eyes caught his as she fell.

The Lost Child

When morning comes as salt and fish, the dream
of fish, a trawler runs against the tide,
slipping the coast to drift its net at sea.
On board, a man who tuned a radio
to catch a country station from the shore
now sings along, and eyes the languid swells
as though he makes discoveries occur
by will. He might believe it: what he sees
on this gray sea—the mirrored gulls and fish,
the sky and water's interchange on each
good day that comes. It's want that brings the fish.
Today he spots a drifting birch—something
he's never seen so far away from shore
a yellow slicker tangled in its limbs.
The water's weight fills the empty arms.

He tries to mend some sense from these stray threads,
imagines how they intertwine, like strands
that cross and hatch his net, imagines he
can trace them to their knot: a child who's lost,
who climbed a tree grappling a bank, then fell—
the *tree* fell—into the sea. So when he spots
the morning's roiling birds and fish, the fray
worrying the horizon's seam, he thinks
he'll find the child, afloat, pummeled by waves.
But no. There is no child. Nothing but salt
and water, gulls and fish embroidering

the air. A shadow runs beneath the boat,
a rising school of fish with eyes like the eyes
of needles, that turns away from the net,
the boat, the want, to stitch against the tide.

Scale Model of Childhood

Who can say what calls me to work
these late hours
by lamplight and magnifying glass?

After the ladybug retracts its long,
knife-point wings
beneath its red shell,

I use a brush of one hair
to connect the black stars
stippled on its back:

Canis Minor,
who licks its teeth,
muzzle still red with Acteon's blood,

Canis Minor,
waiting at the feet of the Twins
for crumbs to fall from their table.

In another room,
my parents sleep lightly,
never dreaming,

mouths open
as though ready always
to call my name.

When my constellation is finished,
I pierce it with a pin,
my little dog,

and place it
in a miniature box,
size of my thumbnail,

a window for the shoe box diorama
I assemble each night
from tidbits no one will miss.

When I was a child
feral dogs ran the woods
beyond our door.

Even the hound my father shot
slipped away by morning,
a line of blood pocking the snow.

My parents instructed me,
never stray outside.
Nights, my back on the bed

and my head tilted back,
I watched stars scroll past
my narrow window's frame.

Once I thought I'd step from childhood
as from a doorway
into a night blazing with stars

so numerous
they defied constellation.
I'd stride into the revealed world

away from the house
and my parents framed by a window
as they sat at a table

holding forks
with no morsels pierced
near parted lips.

Pull the lever on the side of the box
and their forks will scrape
empty plates

while an unseen dog
howls for its dinner
in an almost human voice.

What Fire Wants

She rides the trolley down St. Charles and into the evening,
    staring into the shiver and twist of flames
in the gas lamps, the flickering doorways, and thinks
    the fire's shawl of light strains to open,

until, at last, she sees her father beneath the consummation
    of smoke and dust drifting from a rural road
a few years before he died, the narrow strings of flame
    dragging through the grass, combing

it down, untangling it into ash, into what fire wants of things.
    She wanted to step a little closer, to feel
the tender pulse of heat like the blood ticking the lines
    of her wrist, but her father waved

her back. The fire flushed grackles into the sprawling mesh
    of smoke, and they squelched warnings
the way a radio spits from a car as it turns down a street
    and into the city. But it isn't enough,

the splinter of a song. Or the lamps. No, she wants to tell how
    her father walked into that field, the smoke
draping like muslin walls, until she could see only the taut
    threads of fire and the black birds torn

from gray sheets. But the man slumped next to her glances again
    and again at her hands where they pool

in her lap and she'll tell him nothing, not that her father
    wanted to know how it felt to stand

in the field's unscorched center and watch the closing flames,
    that he left her, a child, to wait and do
nothing but watch him disappear . . . though instead
    of waiting she imagined her father

collecting strands of fire, imagined he tied them into a flashing
    blanket he would bring . . . Now she says
nothing, and slowly shuts her eyes to the flames gesturing
    from the doorways of houses—*stay,*

stay away—and she feels the car filling with grackles.
    They settle on the vacant seats to hunt
for string and thread to weave their nests of what's lost,
    and call out with voices like hinges.

Sparrows

My mother wanted to believe she would never lose me,

the way she wanted to believe in Christ
but now maybe all she believes is Thomas,
how he lost the world when the wound opened
to his finger. Thomas knew then
the world changes when the sleeper's eyes turn

into his head and open, dreaming. In his dream
the spear splits Christ's skin and splits his heart
irrevocably, so grief can be real and not faith's failure.
But Christ returned, Thomas traced a finger through the gash
and knew faith and the world conspired against him.

And I want to believe, staring into a tree's branches
where sparrows wake hours before the light,
in how the sparrows' chorus seems one voice
layered over and over itself—
birds so similar they could all be refractions of one bird,

shattered into a hundred selves
as I would shatter, into past and present, into two lives,
to be both child and man rather than the neither I am.
I want to walk into the house and sleep at my lover's back.
I want to stand on the rock in the river where I stood numbly

as a child, my mother looking on from a bridge,
watching my foot twist down the rock's slick face
into the current I thought wanted only to carry itself away.
If I could draw my foot back and suspend the moment
a few years . . . but then,

the water simply opened like a wound
and took me in. So I believe in dissolution, my heart's vagueness
in wanting everything. Or rather, how through the cover of limbs
and leaves I glimpse only the drab flashings
of sparrows and nothing whole,

unlike Thomas who saw their entirety on a roadside.
He left Christ and the crowding Apostles
and walked to where those few sparrows fluttered in the dirt,
dusting their bodies, preening sand into ruffled feathers,
and he thought then if he ever slept what was real would slip

from him to drift in sleep, and the world would reveal itself
changed and inconstant. Or he might simply dissolve into dust,
this dust, a patina on the sparrows' backs.
And when another boy pulled me from the river
my mother already knew she'd lost me. I would disappear into
    myself

if she watched, if she didn't.

Littoral

The man in the car next to me, jammed
in the fuss of traffic merging onto a highway
that arches over another, reads a Bible

propped against his steering wheel as he waits.
He must believe he can choose between worlds—
a heaven arching beyond the blackness in the air,

and his skin that smells slightly like earth.
A page, as he turns it, rustles with the sound
of wings, and an itch unfurls across his back.

But I watch the cars on the highway bleed along
below. Their lights become the streaming iridescence
of jellyfish spinning in an oval-faced tank

I saw once, papery shells backlit so they glowed
above neon-pulsed tendrils, bodies furling into wings
to trace their world's perimeter against the glass.

\~

A friend once described a street fountain
capped by the Annunciation—Mary with her palms
accepting the angel's words, his revision of her body,

the inscription of transcendence into her flesh.
She told me a man leaned against the fountain,
playing saxophone with hands so like her dead father's

she would have sworn they were his—one index a nub,
a finger hacked away when she was ten.
His other fingers circled that emptiness,

inscribing the saxophone's dull length
with a trope of presence and absence,
the way streaming light twines with water

in the fountain, and brilliant tendrils waver
between light and flesh,
like the valence of body and language.

•••〜

I didn't leave when she turned
from telling me more to walk back to her car
and the highway that would wash her

into the city, toward whatever solace
she carved for herself above the traffic's girded hum
in the yellowed walls of her apartment.

I kept to the beach.
When I found a gelatinous bubble, milky,
solid to my toe's prodding, its hair of tendrils

plucked by waves on the uncertain seam between water
and shore, it had already begun its transformation,
the sand washing in, settling over it, a page.

71

Soup

i

I begin in the particular: this thin fan of steam
whisking the air as it rises from a bowl of soup,
today's *Almuerzo*—an orange broth so flecked with beans

hinged to their own dissolution it mimics the walls
of this place, flaking into their past. And in the middle
of the bowl, nudged by the spoon's curve,

a piece of gristle clings to a bone fragment,
still not yielding its final semblance of the body.
Begin here, as good a place as any, my head

bowing to meet the spoon's graze against
my pale lips, my image, reversed, blooming
across the nicks and scratches in the burnished metal.

My back is turned to the open door
and the city in celebration, the whirl of voices
shouting from the street in another language,

the alternating horn blasts, traces of music—
the voicings of a city that neither wants me
nor needs me to go on with its reveling.

Here I seem more distinct than anywhere else
because here I begin unraveling, not with pain
but with a numbness that drifts from where my spine

first gives way, even as I fade into invisibility:
the waitress brings a plate of rice and beans
and *platanos,* and setting it on the table

she looks through me, her eyes incising a line
to the open door and the multiplying crowd,
the city's dense and discordant image of her life.

ii

When I went to look for this country's beginnings
in the Monasterio de las Conceptas de Cuenca
I found a colonial carving of Christ, life-sized,

peering from the wall of a small room
with beaten, blued eyes that could own at best
only pinpricks of vision, blood trapped in paralytic flow

from grooves rent in the body, thick washes of red
cracked and curling away from the pocked forehead's
yellow skin, from each thorn's bite,

blood flaking from the spike driven into one hand,
so that there, in the impossible resolve of knuckles,
I could see woodgrain and a splintering worm track

that submitted again to the paint's gloss
but was the twitch of its undoing. On the wall
a plaque proclaimed this *El Jesús del Gran Poder,*

and withheld its maker's name, denying the history
of hands that shaped Christ's body, that claimed a piece
of the New World and rived it away, into the Old.

iii

But this city sustains itself, beyond the door
of the *restaurante,* sustains constant discord, the wheel
of voices in flux but always spinning,

roiling the celebrants into itself: the street musician calling
"Cante, cante," to a woman who laughs and begins to sing
in the midst of the ongoing song; the thief

who grunts to himself as he slashes the straps of a bag
with his small razor and strips possessions
from one of an undifferentiated line of backs

as though trimming fat from a piece of meat;
the young men shouting from a balcony as they toss
water-gorged balloons into the milling crowds

with the same smooth gesture as the cook's,
casting chunks of muscle and bone into the broth
through the fanning steam's erasure in air.

iv.

Months after I leave this table, this city,
a doctor will stick a needle into my arm,
and I'll count my way into blankness, into surface,

until I too am muscle, bone, and gristle
husking a dreamlessness. Then she'll split
the skin of my back—*this* blood drawn by tubes—

spread and pin my muscles into a yawn
and pick away the shattered spinal disc,
coaxing the pieces from my body's wiring

the way a monastery curator pulls
worms, fattened on Christ's diminishment,
from the wooden body . . . Until I cease being

an operation. *It was a soup in there,*
she'll say—she couldn't find every shard.
And worms still fret the carving with absence,

thinning it inside so I could crack its arm
open with the rap of my knuckle. But for now
I work meat from the bone and ignore the waitress

trailing her fingers along the peeled doorframe,
and the cook's small sounds clamoring from the kitchen,
even the reveler, paused at the window, who grins,

not at me but at himself, at his hair
he's painted red, at rivulets of sweat
streaking his face with dye, at the violin

perched on his shoulder, two strings frayed
into silence. I chew the meat, gnash my teeth
through the gristle that marries its unmaking

to what sustains. I am becoming myself.

Notes

"Solace": Franz Xaver Kappus is the young poet addressed in Rainer Maria Rilke's *Letters to a Young Poet*.

"Elegy for the Music": The epigraph quotes Eric Dolphy's closing words from the album *Last Date*.

"Gislebertus": The twelfth-century craftsman famous for distinctive sculptures which adorn St. Lazare Cathedral in France, and for the fact that he prominently signed his work, an unprecedented act for a sculptor of his era.

"American Monochrome": The italicizied phrase comes from a note written by Franz Kafka during his final illness. While undergoing treatment for tuberculosis, Kafka received orders not to speak, and so communicated by means of what Max Brod later called "Conversation Slips." This note is included in Kafka's *Letters to Friends, Family and Editors*, translated by Richard and Clara Winston.

"The Wrong Story": Lines 6 through 9 adapt material from Warner Wells's translation of Michihiko Hachiya's *Hiroshima Diary*.

"For Keats, after Keats": Nearly fifty of John Keats's letters survive only in copies made from lost originals. Some copyists remained true to the originals, making only minor changes to correct spelling, punctuation, and capitalization. Other copyists—notably, brother-in-law John Jeffrey and friend Charles Brown—made more significant alterations. Brown's cautious and protective attitude toward Keats's legacy led him to eliminate names and omit passages from the correspondence he transcribed, as is the case with the poet's final letter.

Illinois Poetry Series
Laurence Lieberman, Editor

History Is Your Own Heartbeat
Michael S. Harper (1971)

The Foreclosure
Richard Emil Braun (1972)

The Scrawny Sonnets and Other
  Narratives
Robert Bagg (1973)

The Creation Frame
Phyllis Thompson (1973)

To All Appearances: Poems New
  and Selected
Josephine Miles (1974)

The Black Hawk Songs
Michael Borich (1975)

Nightmare Begins Responsibility
Michael S. Harper (1975)

The Wichita Poems
Michael Van Walleghen (1975)

Images of Kin: New and Selected
  Poems
Michael S. Harper (1977)

Poems of the Two Worlds
Frederick Morgan (1977)

Cumberland Station
Dave Smith (1977)

Tracking
Virginia R. Terris (1977)

Riversongs
Michael Anania (1978)

On Earth as It Is
Dan Masterson (1978)

Coming to Terms
Josephine Miles (1979)

Death Mother and Other Poems
Frederick Morgan (1979)

Goshawk, Antelope
Dave Smith (1979)

Local Men
James Whitehead (1979)

Searching the Drowned Man
Sydney Lea (1980)

With Akhmatova at the Black Gates
Stephen Berg (1981)

Dream Flights
Dave Smith (1981)

More Trouble with the Obvious
Michael Van Walleghen (1981)

The American Book of the Dead
Jim Barnes (1982)

The Floating Candles
Sydney Lea (1982)

Northbook
Frederick Morgan (1982)

Collected Poems, 1930-83
Josephine Miles (1983; reissue, 1999)

The River Painter
Emily Grosholz (1984)

Healing Song for the Inner Ear
Michael S. Harper (1984)

The Passion of the Right-Angled Man
T. R. Hummer (1984)

Dear John, Dear Coltrane
Michael S. Harper (1985)

Poems from the Sangamon
John Knoepfle (1985)

In It
Stephen Berg (1986)

The Ghosts of Who We Were
Phyllis Thompson (1986)

Moon in a Mason Jar
Robert Wrigley (1986)

Lower-Class Heresy
T. R. Hummer (1987)

Poems: New and Selected
Frederick Morgan (1987)

Furnace Harbor: A Rhapsody of the
    North Country
Philip D. Church (1988)

Bad Girl, with Hawk
Nance Van Winckel (1988)

Blue Tango
Michael Van Walleghen (1989)

Eden
Dennis Schmitz (1989)

Waiting for Poppa at the Smithtown
    Diner
Peter Serchuk (1990)

Great Blue
Brendan Galvin (1990)

What My Father Believed
Robert Wrigley (1991)

Something Grazes Our Hair
S. J. Marks (1991)

Walking the Blind Dog
G. E. Murray (1992)

The Sawdust War
Jim Barnes (1992)

The God of Indeterminacy
Sandra McPherson (1993)

Off-Season at the Edge of the World
Debora Greger (1994)

National Poetry Series

Eroding Witness
Nathaniel Mackey (1985)
Selected by Michael S. Harper

Palladium
Alice Fulton (1986)
Selected by Mark Strand

Cities in Motion
Sylvia Moss (1987)
Selected by Derek Walcott

The Hand of God and a Few
Bright Flowers
William Olsen (1988)
Selected by David Wagoner

The Great Bird of Love
Paul Zimmer (1989)
Selected by William Stafford

Stubborn
Roland Flint (1990)
Selected by Dave Smith

The Surface
Laura Mullen (1991)
Selected by C. K. Williams

The Dig
Lynn Emanuel (1992)
Selected by Gerald Stern

My Alexandria
Mark Doty (1993)
Selected by Philip Levine

The High Road to Taos
Martin Edmunds (1994)
Selected by Donald Hall

Theater of Animals
Samn Stockwell (1995)
Selected by Louise Glück

The Broken World
Marcus Cafagña (1996)
Selected by Yusef Komunyakaa

Nine Skies
A. V. Christie (1997)
Selected by Sandra McPherson

Lost Wax
Heather Ramsdell (1998)
Selected by James Tate

So Often the Pitcher Goes to Water un-
   til It Breaks
Rigoberto González (1999)
Selected by Ai

Renunciation
Corey Marks (2000)
Selected by Philip Levine

Other Poetry Volumes

Local Men and Domains
James Whitehead (1987)

Her Soul beneath the Bone:
  Women's Poetry on Breast Cancer
Edited by Leatrice Lifshitz (1988)

Days from a Dream Almanac
Dennis Tedlock (1990)

Working Classics: Poems on
  Industrial Life
Edited by Peter Oresick and Nicholas
  Coles (1990)

Hummers, Knucklers, and Slow
  Curves: Contemporary Baseball Po
  ems
Edited by Don Johnson (1991)

The Double Reckoning of Christopher
  Columbus
Barbara Helfgott Hyett (1992)

Selected Poems
Jean Garrigue (1992)

New and Selected Poems, 1962-92
Laurence Lieberman (1993)

The Dig and Hotel Fiesta
Lynn Emanuel (1994)

For a Living: The Poetry of Work
Edited by Nicholas Coles and Peter
  Oresick (1995)

The Tracks We Leave: Poems on En-
  dangered Wildlife of North America
Barbara Helfgott Hyett (1996)

Peasants Wake for Fellini's Casanova
  and Other Poems
Andrea Zanzotto; edited and translated
  by John P. Welle and Ruth Feldman;
  drawings by Federico Fellini and Au-
  gusto Murer (1997)

Moon in a Mason Jar and What My
  Father Believed
Robert Wrigley (1997)

The Wild Card: Selected Poems,
  Early and Late
Karl Shapiro; edited by Stanley Kunitz
  and David Ignatow (1998)

Turtle, Swan and Bethlehem in Broad
  Daylight
Mark Doty (2000)

Typeset in 10.5/14 Veljovic
with Thymesans display
Designed by Paula Newcomb
Composed by Celia Shapland
for the University of Illinois Press
Manufactured by Thomson-Shore, Inc.

University of Illinois Press
1325 South Oak Street
Champaign, IL 61820-6903
www.press.uillinois.edu